PROJECT FLOP

Good Lessons From A Bad Teacher

A book about failures

by

Ian Sands

Project Flop: Good lesson From A Bad Teacher

Copyright © 2014 Ian Sands

Written by Ian Sands

Cover Photo by Craig Roland

ACKNOWLEDGMENTS

There are so many people to thank for making this book possible. Everyone from my high school art teachers to the principals who gave me the opportunities. Of course, an art teacher isn't much without his students so a big shout out to all of them.. well, most of them.. JK!

Dedicated to Mrs. Carolyn Royal
for giving me the opportunity

Project : *Flop*

good lessons from a bad teacher

a book about failures
by ian sands

Ian Sands

Photos of many of the failed projects in this book can be found

online at:

http://iansands.weebly.com

Intro:

Let's Get Ready To Rumble!

The only class I ever failed in college was Intro to Art Education. If you put this book down and stop reading right now I will totally understand. If you keep reading, you will learn that over the years, I've frequently clashed and often collided and have had plenty of failures in the world of art education.

My college, The School of Visual Arts (SVA) is located on 23rd Street on the island of Manhattan. As the course title suggests, Intro to Art Education was designed to provide those considering a possible career as an art educator a look at the process. I can't truly remember why I enrolled in the class. I can only assume I had fond memories of being in my high school art class and saw this as an avenue back. I soon would learn there would be no nostalgia.

I don't recall ever meeting in a classroom on SVA's facilities. I do remember meeting at a local elementary school. There, the course instructor taught a lesson to the elementary school children while her college students (including me) watched her teach. After the lesson, when the elementary students had left the room, we would discuss, evaluate, and critique the events of the day.

Eventually, I believe the students would be preparing our own lessons and taking turns teaching the class. I use the word "believe" because I never found out. I stopped going to class. I stopped going because I didn't understand the "edu-speak" the teacher used. Words like curriculum and standards. I stopped going because none of this was creative or experimental or fun. I stopped going because I came to the realization that art education was about objectives and summaries and not about art at all. At least, that's what I thought.

I went to student services to withdraw from the class. I was informed that it was too late. The deadline to drop a class without it being on my permanent record had passed. If I didn't return to class, I would fail.

Fail? What did I care? Art education was not for me. There were plenty of other art careers to choose from. I didn't need to worry about failing this class because I would never, ever become an art teacher.

To this day, if you review my transcripts, right there in the middle of the page, under the line spring -1985 it reads: Course AE202 Intro To Art Education Grade: F Quality Points 0.00. But as I mentioned, this was not the last time I would toe the line with failure. There were more battles to be fought and more fights to battle. Let's get ready to rumble!

Book One: The Flops

"I can not take credit for my student's successes if I don't
first take credit for their failings."

~ Ian Sands

A Book About Failures?

All project start off with the best intentions. Whether you
create the lesson from scratch or borrow it from someone
else, in your mind you envision success. You write your
lesson trying to plan for every situation that may arise.
The supplies are laid out, a presentation and a demo are
reviewed and practiced, and everything should go off
without a hitch. Then, be it fate, a misalignment of the

7

planets or perhaps the art gods are angry, the lesson falls apart. Regardless of your preparation the students don't understand. As for your enthusiasm, the class simply doesn't share your zeal for the project. You try to pull it all together but in the end, for lack of a better word, it fails. Worse off, you take it personally. You feel like you failed. You will be happy to know that you're in good company.

Good teachers fail. Great teachers fail, a lot. Yes, I'm sure you can find a teacher who will proudly tell you her projects never fail. There are those teachers that have a set of fail-proof projects that they do over and over again. However, even these teachers at one time had a few failures before they cast their lesson plan book in bronze. These teachers might not fail but they also never take chances, never try new things and therefore never grow. Good teachers fail because they are willing to step out of their comfort zone to better their programs. Great teachers fail a lot because they are constantly learning and developing and are passionate about sharing what they learn.

You are probably familiar with the story that states that Thomas Edison failed more than 1,000 times when trying to find the right filament for the light bulb. When asked about it, Edison supposedly said, "I have not failed 1,000 times. I have successfully discovered 1,000 ways to NOT make a light bulb." Through this story we are to gain the understanding that, even when we fail, we still learn. That to fail is not truly failure.

Some of the projects I currently attempt with my art classes don't work well. One in particular, a photography assignment called forced perspective, stands out. The concept is to have students take photographs of objects at different distances so that an illusion is created that the closer object is larger than it really is. A soda bottle might be placed close to the camera. A person might then stand several yards behind the soda can. The illusion created is that the person is standing on a giant soda can. This is a fun project to try but rather challenging to complete successfully. I advise my students when attempting this project to take many photos of the same idea. The reason is because for every ten photos they take; only one will come out as they originally planned. Perhaps the person and the soda can will be misaligned or the photographer will think she has it right but doesn't. Whatever the reason, many of those photos won't work. A group of students will return to class with a 100 photos but only ten will be worth viewing. Out of those ten, only three or so will be truly outstanding. Did the project fail 90 times? No, the students just learned 90 ways not to take a forced perspective photograph.

Sometimes a project might not go well but produces an alternative project almost by mistake. I experienced this when conducting a lesson in light drawing. Light drawing, like forced perspective, is one of those projects with a learning curve. It seems easy enough. In a dark room, using a camera with a shutter speed set to stay open for ten seconds, a photo is taken of someone drawing in the air with a glow stick. In theory, the results produce an illuminated line drawing. In practice, for every ten photos take, one decent line image is produced along with nine blotchy, blurry images of streaks of lights.

One time, while failing miserably at producing anything that looked like something, a student picked up a cut out stencil from an older spray painting project. She waved the glow stick behind the stencil while her partner took the photo and voila, the first light graffiti image was captured. As it turns out, capturing quality light graffiti images has a much higher success rate than none stenciled light drawings. As long as the effort is put in ahead of time to produce a quality stencil, capturing a decent image only take one or two tries. I can say with certitude that light graffiti was invented because of the failings of the project it evolved from.

Sometimes projects don't work at all. I read an article online about creating moss graffiti. Not only were there examples of moss graffiti created by some of the best moss graffiti artists, there was a recipe for creating the "paint" that, when applied to a wall, would grow moss. I couldn't pass this up.

I selected a wall where moss was already growing. The class and I talked a little about street art and graffiti before I whipped out the blender. I mixed all the correct ingredients, though some would later argue that I didn't follow the measurements strictly enough, and produced a rather nasty looking concoction. With brushes and cups of full of moss-paint in hand we made our way to the wall. Some students wrote their names or memorable quotes while others created simple drawings. We didn't put too much emphasis on preparing what we would paint. In hindsight I'm glad because the moss never grew. The mixture we created stained the wall but that was about it.

At the end of the semester, I asked my students which project had the least value. The moss graffiti was at the top of the list, primarily because it didn't grow. However, each student whom identified the moss project as a failure was also quick to point out the positives of the project. Overall it was fun, interesting, and a break from being inside. Since the project was conducted at the beginning of the semester, they also sited it as provided an opportunity to get to know each other a little better. The project didn't produce the result we had expected but it produced results.

All three of these project examples failed at some level. Yet, none of them were total failures. In fact, even though the moss project was the most disappointing of the three, I would still consider trying it again. That is because I believe under the right conditions we will not only achieve the success that the students noted, but also be able to produce the intended result of growing moss graffiti. This is not to say a project shouldn't have a limit as to when it should not be tried again. For me, that is when the failure of the desired outcome of the lesson outweighs the project's intentional or unintentional successes. That is to say, all students should meet some level of success.

I used to teach a printing lesson in which the students would draw on cardboard and then add layers of white glue to raise the surface. After many layers of glue, printing ink would be applied and a print created. The drawings had to be large enough to handle the thickness created by the layer. It took several days of layering the glue before it was ready for printing. Though each student was able to produce the intended outcome, the end results were less than impressive. Unlike the moss project, there were no unintentional successes. This project was time consuming and the students found it tedious and boring. Furthermore, they were frustrated and dissatisfied with their own art. For me, this was the definition of a failed project and one that need not be tried again.

In the next few chapters I will introduce you to the best of my failed projects. Although they all failed on some level, they all had some unintentional successes. Let the

Project Flop:

failing begin.

.....

Ian Sands

Monalloon

One of my favorite classes to teach is Art History. It is special to me. I only teach it once a year and it's always a great group of kids who enroll. I give many project-based assignments, usually starting with small individual projects that eventually lead up to large, group projects. Examples of smaller projects include designing art history based kites and games. A larger group project example would be designing a class miniature golf course. For this assignment, teams of students are tasked with creating a fully functional artist based mini golf course hole. At the conclusion of the assignment, all the holes are set up in the courtyard along with clubs and golf balls. The entire school is invited to play the course.

I like to end the year with one large project that the whole class can participate in at once. In example, previously we have created several art history based videos. One year we shot a remake of the Hold Your Horses art history inspired video titled, 70 Million. The students lip-dubbed the song while dressed up as recreations of famous artworks. The video came out great, but I still thought we had one larger project in us. I wanted a project that would out do any project we had done before or probably would do again. I came up with the best idea in the world. A giant replica of the Mona Lisa created out of balloons. The Monalloon!

In theory the Monalloon was brilliant. A clear reference, created in Photoshop, would guide the placement of the more than 1,800 balloons. Working with my top notch art history class student advisors, we decided the best way to keep the balloons in place would be to create a giant 40' x 46' grid in the parking lot. The grid would be composed of string that would be tied together every ten inches. One balloon would be held in place at the intersection where each horizontal and vertical string met. On paper, this project was flawless.

Each student in class brought in a bag of balloons. On the day of the Monalloon's assembly the balloons were separated into piles by color. Meanwhile, a group of students went to the parking lot and created the string grid. When the grid was assembled, everyone started blowing up balloons and carrying them outside. Operation Monalloon was under way!

Our first half hour was very promising. Though we had completed only a few rows of balloons, it was apparent that it would look like something. Then, something went slightly wrong. There was a light breeze and a balloon popped. One of the girls ran back to the art room, retrieved the same color balloon and replaced it. Before she could tie it down, there was another breeze and another balloon popped. She called out for someone to replace it. One of the boys, who was coming out with his next balloon surrendered it as the replacement. He went back inside to get another balloon. Before he could return, two more balloons had popped. Another slight breeze and several more balloons popped. It wasn't long before we were losing two balloons for everyone carried out. We were only an hour into the project and we were further behind than we had been only a half ago previously.

What we didn't realize at the time was that tiny particles of sand covered the parking lot. Every time the breeze blew, it lifted a row of the balloons. As the balloons settled back down on the lot they would meet these microscopic bits of glass and ... Pop! My students started to realize the futility of continuing. I, on the other hand, had been blinded by my desire to see the project come to fruition. We had planned it all out so well. I thought if we could only blow up the balloons faster.. or something .. Anything. It wasn't long till the entire class was back in the trailer and I was sitting on the curb staring at a deflated dream.

This project failed, but not for reasons that didn't have solutions. Sometime later, when we were no longer feeling flat, a team of students sat down to discuss lessons learned. A list of improvements was developed. These included a better grid design, more students working on the project and most importantly, a covering for the parking lot. Everything was duly noted, even though I knew I wouldn't attempt such a foolhardy task again.

Six months later, I was contacted by Craig Roland, professor at the University of Florida. He was roaming the country interviewing art teachers about their use of technology in the classroom and wanted to stop by Apex High for a visit. I readily agreed and we set a date.
"I hope you have something big planned for when I get there," He said.
"Oh, yes," I responded. "I have something in mind."
The Monalloon!

Whether a project is successful or not, there can always be a "lesson learned'. Gaining that knowledge is interesting. Applying that information, and turning a failed project into a success is priceless! In November of 2010 we did just that.

Our first applied 'lesson learned' was designing and implementing a better grid. Instead of simply laying string on the parking lot, we constructed a frame of 2' x 2' wooden beams. The beams would keep the string grid off the ground. Screws were drilled into the wood every ten inches and twine was tied to each nail. I can tell you that nobody is happier than a high school student with a power tool in their hand.

Our second improvement was to enlist the help of all the Art One classes. We increased the number of students from 30 to 190. Coordinating seven classes and three teachers was a task in and of itself. In order to do so, the project was directed by one student who was in charge of the master Mona Lisa design. As chief operations officer, she directed a team of managers who gave directions to all the other students. Everyone had to know what color balloon they needed to inflate and where that particular balloon had to go. This was perhaps the most successful part of the project and one that was totally student lead.

Third, and perhaps most importantly, we covered the parking lot with table cloths borrowed from the Sculpture class. These were originally intended to use when working on ceramic projects. Instead, they prevented the previous popping problem. The stage was set.

The morning of November 19th was clear and cold. Craig Roland captured the moment on camera as the coordination of the balloons began. The rows filled quickly and few, if any balloons popped. However, I soon realized that even with the addition of six more art classes, this project was going to take far longer than I had ever expected. It ran all morning, through lunch and into the afternoon. I had to leave the scene to attend to my Computer Art class on the other side of the campus. It wasn't till about ten minutes before the end of the school day that I received a call on the computer lab phone, "It's done. You've got to see this."

By the time I reached the site, students from all over campus were there taking photographs. I myself grabbed a camera and headed to the third floor of the adjacent building. There, to the dismay of that classroom teacher, I found several yearbook photographers literally hanging out the window trying to get a good shot. It wasn't perfect, but it was pretty cool. How can a 40' x 46' Mona Lisa made entirely out of balloons not be cool?

Since that day I've been asked by students if I would do this again. In hindsight, they see the "wow" factor but there is no way they can see the struggle, the heartache, the innovation or the incredible coordination that went into the creation of that project. I'm not quite sure I'll ever be ready to go through all that again. Then again, maybe someday, I will.

.....

Chalk Mural Graffiti

Chalk murals get a bad rap. At least, that has been my experience working in education. I don't see it happening anywhere else. The City of Raleigh puts on a street chalk festival every year where people of all ages get a chance to spread pastels on Fayetteville Street. Julian Beever, an English street artist, went viral on the Internet with his anamorphic chalk drawings. My email has received countless messages all claiming, "Unbelievable Street Art!" filling my box with images of his work. Still, it isn't uncommon to hear comments about how a lesson in sidewalk chalk will only lead to school wide graffiti. This type of discussion I'm used to. The conversation I had one afternoon with the creative writing teacher was a little different.

The creative writing teacher is a year older than retirement age. She is hands down one of the sweetest, kind-hearted teachers I know. As I learned, she can be brutally honest in her opinions but not with malicious intent. She is in no way tech savvy or current on trends. She is what you might call, old school. Though any of this could be used against her, there isn't a student or teacher at school that would talk ill of her.

I should mention that the project I'll describe was very successful. Teams of students developed interactive chalk drawings that adorn the outside walls of our school's courtyard. The concept was simple and fun. Each wall mural would be missing one major element; a place where a participant would stand so a photograph could be taken. The participant would then be magically transported into the art. One example was a drawing of a giant pencil hovering over a math quiz. When a participant stood beneath the pencil with lifted arms it gave the illusion that the person was holding the pencil. Other murals provided spaces for dragons to be fought, marshmallows to be roasted and even a roller coaster to be rode.

On the last day of the project I was standing in the
courtyard watching the students, cellphones in hands,
snapping photos of their friends inserted in the art. At that
moment the creative writing teacher walked up and stood
next to me. I won't lie, I was in my glory. As you know
by reading this book, not all my plans work out so
successfully so I was extra excited at how well this one
had gone. I leaned over and asked her what she thought,
expecting the obvious praise the students and I deserved.

"I hate it," she said.

I was shocked. How could anyone hate this project? It
was so colorful and playful. I could only imagine she
didn't understand the concept. I started to explain but she
stopped me. It wasn't the project she had an issue with. It
wasn't even these walls or this art. She proceeded to
share with me what I couldn't see in the murals. I will try
my best to explain it here.

She grew up in the post World War II Germany. As a

child, she had seen the bombed buildings of Berlin. She understood on a very personal level the devastating affect war has on a person, on a country and on the world. The ruins of those German buildings stood as a monument; a reminder of the pain and suffering that she had experienced in her life.

In the 1980's, a new generation was taking over the streets of Germany. With the fall of the Berlin wall, graffiti artists were free to go back and forth coloring the walls of bombed out churches and war-torn buildings. Since that time, the ever growing street art movement has completely changed the urban landscape from that of a monument of destruction to a celebration of life. Many would find this transformation exciting. The creative writing teacher saw it differently.

For her, the new generation spray painted over the grave site of a fallen city. She sees it less as a celebration of color and more as an act of disrespect. Not deliberately. Perhaps out of ignorance. Each stroke of an artist's spray can erases a bit more of the memory.

When the creative writing teacher looked at the courtyard covered in chalk, she didn't see an exciting, interactive art lesson. She saw a reminder of something she wants us to never forget. The interactive chalk mural was not a failed project, though for the creative writing teacher, it failed to produce the results we had sought. It did however, give me insight and a new perspective that I will certainly share with future students. And that after all, is what art should be all about.

.....

Ian Sands

Cup Portrait Project

I'm sure you have heard the old saying, it is better to ask forgiveness than ask permission. I tend to lean in that direction. It is helpful that my administration is so supportive of the arts. They've never put up any roadblocks as my class has roamed the school, armed with whatever medium is on the agenda and looking for a spot to create a masterpiece. My administration is supportive. Mother Nature on the other hand is not always so tolerant.

The Cup Portrait Project, pre-mother nature, was flawless. As the name suggests, the objective was to create a portrait using only cups and a fence. To make sure the concept was plausible; I created a test reference by combining two photographs. First, I took a picture of the chain link fencing that ran behind my art trailer. Although I hadn't gone back and examined the fencing up close and in person, I could see that it was tall and had enough sections where several teams of students could work. Next, I snagged a photo of Keith Haring off the Internet.

In Photoshop, I placed the Haring photo as a layer on top of the fence image. Swapping the layer mode to multiply enabled me to see the fence through the photo. Using the paint bucket tool, I carefully selected and filled in selected holes of the fence to represent where the cups would be placed. When I was finished, I turned off the Haring Photo layer. This left me with the perfect reference for a cup portrait.

Even though they would be working in teams, I wanted all my students to participate in the reference creation process. My goal was twofold. My first reason was noble. I wanted to give every student the opportunity to learn the technology. My second motive was to ensure that every team had a decent reference to work from. Believing that the front end of this project was going to be the only roadblock to a series of effective cup portraits, I wanted the class to have as many successful references to choose from as possible. The class spent a period in the computer lab. After viewing a short tutorial on the process, each student was able to create their own cup portrait reference.

Back in the art room, I taped a printout of each cup portrait reference to the board. I let the class vote on the top five images they thought were most successful. The top five winners then became   team captains. Like a game of kickball in the school yard, I let each captain take a turn at selecting who would be on their team. I was setting up this project to be fail proof. We had the highest quality references and five teams of artists all selected by the students. The front end was done, the hard part completed. Now it would simply be a matter of placing the cups in the fence. Or so I thought.

The next day we went outside so each group could select a section of fencing. It had rained the night before so the ground was wet. Also, the overgrown bushes and shrubs around the fence were wet too. We trampled though the overgrowth and reached the fencing.

Once there, we encountered another obstacle. What had appeared from a distance to be small sprouts and leaves sticking though the fencing turned out to be thick vines. I went back to the trailer and retrieved three saws. The students started cutting and cutting but the amount of vines, which were hopelessly entwined in the fencing, seemed to be endless. Students tugged and yanked and did their best to clear the fence and surrounding area. The entire day was spent ridding the area of brush. Now that it was complete, I thought the rest of the project should go smoothly.

That night it rained again. Not only was the shrubbery wet but the ground was saturated. To reach the fencing we had to go around large puddles and slippery mud slicks. Furthermore, it was colder than it had been the day before. The teams didn't let any of this put a damper on their spirits. They brought with them stacks of cups and their references and started sticking cups in the fence.

This proved trickier than anticipated. First, there were plenty of vines still in the fence. This made inserting the cups rather challenging. Second, the students were having difficulty following their references. Several groups started, then stopped and restarted. The day ended with the class having nothing to show for it.

Day three was worse. Not only did it rain again that night but a light mist was still falling. If the temperature hadn't actually dropped, the rain made it seem as if it had. The teams were still having trouble following the references. To make matters worse, some students started acting out. They made a game of knocking other group's cups out of the fencing. Cold and frustrated, small bands of students made their way back to the trailer. A few students remained but without an entire group they were incapable of completing what had now become a daunting task. I decided to pull the plug. We abandoned the fence, cups and all. The next day we started a new assignment.

The forsaken project lay like a fallen ruin from antiquity.

Clumps of cups, scattered through the fence line was a reminder to all who past of the terrible days wasted on the cup portrait project. After a few weeks I finally went back to the fence with a small group of students to clear the ground and pick any remaining cups out of the fence.

I recently told this story to my latest group of Art One students. They thought the project sounded like fun. They assured me that they could make it work. You may think I'm crazy but I believed them. I believe the project can work. All it needs is the enthusiasm of a team of student who believe they can accomplish the task. That, and a little help from Mother Nature. Who knows, by the time this book is published, I may have already attempted this project again. As you sit there reading this, there might be an image of a successful cup portrait already pinned to Pinterest.

.....

Skittle Art

Quiet often, I'll have a friend let me know about a sale that's going on at the local art supply shop. Usually it's a bargain like a buy-one-get-one free paint tube or canvas deal. Though I'm always grateful when friends are willing to share their findings, their information mostly falls on deaf ears. That is because whenever I shop for my personal art supplies, I like to go to Home Depot or Lowe's. I'd rather have a gallon of house paint than a tube of oil. Give me a sheet of installation foam board over illustration board any day.

My preference for using nontraditional supplies to create art often extends into my teaching curriculum. Obviously, balloons, mud and birdseed are not the typical art room supply closet staple. While it can be fun to experiment with non traditional media, it can also be difficult to determine how much of a particular material will be needed for a lesson. With traditional materials, I can determine the amount of product needed based either on my own previous experience or by asking a fellow art teacher. With nontraditional materials, this simply is not the case. I learned this the hard way when my class attempted the creation of expressive Skittle portraits.

Since every aspect of this assignment was taken from a previous lesson, completing this project successfully should have been a walk in the park. The year before I taught the same lesson using oil pastels. The objective wouldn't be an issue. The portraits would be expressive. We would utilize the expressive Skittle colors and photograph ourselves making expressive facial gestures. To make sure we had a good range of expressions, I had each student write a list of emotions and then practice with a partner making faces. Everyone picked something different. No problem there.

Creating the references wouldn't be an issue either. We would utilize the same method used when creating our very effective Post-It Note portrait murals. We imported our images into Photoshop and applied a gradient map so we could match the Skittle colors. We also applied the mosaic filter so the photograph would be broken down into tiny units. One trip to the computer lab was all it took for each student to create their reference. All we needed were a few Skittles. I asked everybody to bring in a bag.

Day one was a blast. Bags of Skittles were opened and poured into trays for easy access. References were displayed side by side of the large sheets of cardboard where the final masterpieces were to be completed. With a glue bottle hand, the process was one Skittle on the board, one Skittle in the mouth. Time flew by and the next thing we knew class was over. I looked at the boards expecting to see half finished portraits. To my surprise I found that most students had only completed a row or two. To make matters worse, everyone was out of Skittles. I stopped by the Food Lion on the way home and purchased a few small bags.

The next day went exactly the same. Only this time we had a few visitors. The word was out that Sands' class was making Skittle art. Under the guise that they wanted to see how the project was going, little bands of Skittle thieves raided the room. If this project was going to be successful we would need to keep the door locked. We would also need more Skittles. That night I went to Target and purchased several 2.5 pound bags.

The project dragged on over the rest of the week. Though I could see the portrait's starting to come together, the students had a difficult time seeing it. Their inability to see results only lowered esteem for the project which was already on a roller coaster of emotions. Sugar highs at the first half of class were followed by sugar crashes during the second half of the class. When Skittle trading deals, generated by the need for one color over another failed, arguments erupted. All the while we were constantly running out of Skittles. Furthermore, the stores were running out as well. I had already depleted the Food Lion and Target of their entire stock and was now working my way though Walmart's supply.

At the end of week two, the project had created a class
full of students weary of gluing rows of candy, a bunch of
angry moms tired of their kids asking them to purchase
Skittles, and a hungry mob that circled the trailer waiting
for any chance that the door might open. Still, the
portraits were actually starting to work out. Up close they
looked like rows of colored circles but a photograph the
of work revealed how well they were coming along.
Upon seeing the photographs, many of the student's
became reinvigorated. Though a few decided to give up
entirely, most went on to finish their pieces. Some even
took their work home to make sure it was completed. We
displayed the completed portraits in the media center on a
high shelf just in case any bandits had ideas about eating
our art. Though in the end the assignment turned out
really well, I vowed never to do this project again.

Several months later I received a request to submit a
lesson plan for a contest. Since it was still fairly fresh in

my brain, I decide to enter the Expressive Skittle Portrait project. I laid out the objective, the materials needed, the process, the history... you name it, it was in there. The lesson plan won the contest and I received a class set of Prang markers.

At the end of the lesson plan, I include a lessons learned section which I believe is a fitting way to close this chapter.

Lessons Learned:

I would never do this project again. However, if you are crazy enough to try it, here are a few helpful hints.

1. Gluing down the Skittles is a time consuming process. This project took way longer than I thought it would. However, we made rather large portraits. If I were to do this over again, I would certainly reduce the amount of squares when applying the mosaic filter. Maybe keep it down to 40 x 46.

2. Skittles are not cheap. I spent over $100 buying Skittles and I bought them in bulk bags at Target, and once Target sold out, at Walmart. The students also brought in bags. However, if I were to do this project again, limiting the amount of squares when applying the mosaic filter would also reduce the amount of Skittles required.

3. Skittles attract unwanted visitors. It was amazing how many students from other classes stopped by just to see how things were going during this project. They didn't show that type of curiosity when we were working on value scales. We also had ants. If you leave one Skittle on the floor, an ant will find it. That ant will then call all his ant friends because ants apparently like to share.

.....

Ian Sands

Fear Factor

I'm not a big quiz giver. At least, I'm not for using an exam as a summative assessment. Here is my thinking. In theory, a teacher gives a test at the end of a unit. The students take the exam and write the answers to the questions they know. This produces data that the teacher can supposedly use to determine how much the students have learned.

In reality, the testing has little to do with what the students have covered in the unit. It has become a boiled down version of the information presented. Many students don't care about what they learned (let alone learning) during the unit. Unfortunately, school has become about grades and not about acquiring knowledge. They only want to know what will be on the exam. To facilitate that request, many teachers provide a study guide that the students can use the night before to review (AKA cram) for the test. Information gained quickly is lost just as easily. By the end of the next unit, most students have forgotten what they previously studied. So much for summative assessments.

However, I have discovered another, much more practical use for the quiz. While the students think I'm giving a summative assessment, I'm actually using an exam to make the information stick. I do this using a three part method. First, we review the information that may be on an exam. Second, I give them a quiz and let them cheat all they want. Third, I have them grade each other's quizzes. By the time they reach this point, they have gone over the material so many times that they know it by heart. This method is so effective that I would like to call it fail proof. Of course, that would be wrong.

Though it can be a little campy, one of the best ways to engage students during a review session is though the use of games. I remember my high school biology teacher having a Nerf basketball hoop at the front of the class for such purposes. During my first year of teaching Art History, I tried really hard to think of clever games the class could play. At the time, a TV game show called Fear Factor was popular. I decided to turn one of that show's challenges into a review game.

For those not familiar with the show, Fear Factor challenged adventurous contestants to successful complete stunts most people would be to fearful to attempt. Stunt examples included performing tasks at ridiculous heights, or in deep, cold water or at incredibly fast speeds. The game also usually included a disgusting challenge. This could be anything from having live snakes or cockroaches poured on the contestant to having them eat or drink the vilest substances. For my quiz review, I decided to choose the latter.

The review game rules were simple. On the table at the front of the room was a blender filled with a most disgusting looking concoction. There was a cutting board covered with chopped onion, dog and turtle food and various other nasty items. Taped to the board were pieces of paper that when removed revealed a number ranging from 1/2 to 2. Also on the table were plastic cups.

After signing a release form, willing participants were asked a review question. If they answered correctly they would peel a piece of paper from the board. The number beneath determined how many cups of the nasty looking drink they would have to consume. Their reward for successfully drinking all of the liquid without vomiting was a free question card which they could redeem as a correct answer for any question they didn't know on the quiz.

Now here is what the students didn't see. Previous to the start of class, I mixed a banana that I brought from home, a pint of chocolate milk that I had purchased that morning at the gas station, and some green food coloring in the blender. The onions, dog and turtle food on the table was only for display purposes. None of that went into the blender, though the chunkiness of the banana did add to the illusion that it had.

You might think that students wouldn't even consider playing this game. However, you'd be surprised at what they will do to get a good grade. I didn't have to try very hard to convince a student to go first.

As my first victim approached the front of the class, I directed their attention to the release form. I made a big deal about how important it was for the student to read and sign it. After all, I didn't want to get fired if somebody puked. In reality, the form read as follows.

Fear Factor Waiver

By signing this waiver...

1. Please Play along!

2. It's not dog food or gross, but don't let them know that. Do you really think I would make you eat dog food? OK, maybe I would but I'm telling you

this is just bananas and milk with some food coloring.

3. If you don't drink milk or are allergic to bananas, don't drink this.

4. Please pretend that the drink tastes horrible. It makes the game funnier! Gagging, making icky faces, and acting repulsed are encouraged, however, actual vomit is gross so please, no puking.

If you agree to all the fore mentioned terms, please sign. Good luck!

------------------------ ------------------------

------------------------ ------------------------

------------------------ ------------------------

The first student signed the form and answered the review question correctly. A paper was removed from the board revealing the number one. I poured the mixture. Chunks of banana plopped into the cup. Being the actor that he was, the student fainted disgust. He made weird faces and pretended to gag as he drank the slop. To the amazement of the class, he was able to finish the challenge and receive his reward.

From there on it was easier to convince students to step up to the plate. I was amazed at how well each student went along with the gag. They really made a production of how disgusting it was. Some even pretended they would throw up. Of course none did because actually vomiting was a disqualifier. My students went along so well with the bit. A little too well.

After we had gone through all the review questions, I decided it was time to reveal the joke. I filled a cup with the last of the mixture. Holding it high for all the class to see, I informed them of how it was just chocolate milk and bananas. I read the release form out loud. A sigh of relief went through the crowd. As a final gesture, I put the cup to my lips and took a sip. It was only them that I realized why the class had been such good actors.

A thousand thoughts can go through your mind in second. Had I accidentally put the onions in the cup? Did someone slip in some turtle food while I wasn't looking? What was the reason for the vile taste in my mouth? I stood before the class making the same faces my students had made during the game. Only I wasn't faking it. Neither had they. I thought back to the chocolate milk I had purchased that morning from the gas station. A gas station! Picking up the container, I spun it around in my hands searching for the expiration date. Oh yes, it had expired! Fortunately, nobody actually got sick. Though the milk was bad, it was only slightly sour. It had a funky taste and that was about it.

To this day I still play this game though I always test the milk before I pour. The story of the sour milk also makes the end of the game twice as fun. The lesson learned was simple. Never buy chocolate milk from a gas station.

.....

Ian Sands

Broken Kites

Sometimes one seemingly insignificant item can mess up an entire project. Your lesson plan is complete, you have all the materials needed, and everything seems in order. It's not till you actually run through the project for the first time that you realize that one little thing makes a huge difference. Such was the case of the Art History Kite project.

March comes in like a lion and after having been cooped up all winter in a musky classroom, I thought it would be fun to take the Art History class outside and let them feel the wind in their hair. What better way to do that than by flying kites. The Art History kite project was born.

I let the class team up in pairs to design their kites. I gave them a long list of artists to consider but let them chose which artist they wanted to represent. I did have one exception. No Jackson Pollock kites. The "No Jackson

Pollock" rule is usually in effect for all my Art History projects. It's a lot of fun but a little too easy to start tossing paint and call it a day. I like my students to put a little more thought and effort into their work. No offense to Mr. Pollock.

Building a kite is fairly simple. With the exception of the wooden dowels, we had most of the supplies already. The big, colorful bulletin board paper that all schools use worked well for building both the body of the kites as well as the tails. We had lots of tempera paint in which to replicate the students chosen masterpiece. I stopped by Lowe's Hardware the night before construction and purchased enough dowels for each group to have two. The only added supply was the bag of Cheetos one group brought in to glue to their kite. That team decided to honor the installation artist Sandy Skoglund, know for covering a room in the aforementioned snack food.

We had a wide variety of artists represented. Besides Team Cheeto's Skoglund kite there was a Haring, a Dali, a Magritte, a Kline and a Van Gogh to name a few.

The day selected for flying was perfect for kites. Gusts of wind were coming out of the west at 25 miles an hour. Actually, I'm kidding. I don't have any clue what the wind speed was that day but it didn't matter. This class was ready to fly some kites.

We went where any respectful Art History class would go to fly kites; the football field. It was there that we were met by the head coach.

"Who said you could use the field?" he asked.

"Nobody," I admitted.

"Well, you're not supposed to use the field. It could get messed up."

I didn't say it out loud but I'm pretty certain my facial expression matched what I was thinking. You'll let a 300 pound linebacker in cleats run up and down this field but you're worried about a 95 pound art student with a kite?

"Well," He caved. "I guess its ok this one time."

The first flight attempt would be monumental. We all
gather round as Erin prepared for lift off. She let out a
little slack and a light breeze lifted her kite ten feet into
the air. Then an unthinkable tiny little thing happened.
Snap! The one seemingly insignificant item turned out to
be the wooden dowels. When I purchased them, there had
been so many different thicknesses to choose from. I
knew we didn't want anything too thick. Thick dowels
would be too heavy for lift off. Unfortunately, my
mistake of purchasing the lighter dowels was now going
to be the cause of fifteen kite travesties.

One after another the sound of snapping kite dowels was
heard across the football field. All the time and effort that
the students put into creating such wonderful art with the
dream of flight, crushed, or in this case, snapped. All
except for the Cheetos kite. That group had hot glued so
many Cheetos to that kite it was never going to fly.

I thought for sure the class was going to pack it in. I

started walking back towards the school building. The class had other plans. They headed to the opposite end of the field. I could hear Michael screaming as the teams lined up in the end zone.

"Flyers take your Mark! Set!" Dramatic pause. "Fly your kites!"

With that, 15 kids ran down the field in a futile but hysterical attempt at a kite flying race. Most kites crashed and burned before they had left the ten yard line. That didn't stop anyone. This was a race after all and a race should be won! Broken kites tumbled and bounced down the field, dragged along by the determined students.

Apparently, broken kites doesn't equate to broken spirits. That was my take away. Since that class, I've done this lesson a half dozen times. Though I've improved on the dowels, we've very rarely gotten the kites to fly. Still, this is one of those classic projects that in some ways is made more successful by its failures. A flying kite would be memorable. A broken kite is unforgettable.

The Only Real Failure

Of all the projects in the book, despite how horrible the result might have been, regardless of how distant the ending was from the intended result, there were no true failures. I would argue this point because even when the students became totally disillusioned, they understood the reasons for the project's demise and could often sight lessons learned. They knew, as did I, that if a project were ever to be tried again, it might in fact become successful. To be a true failure would be for the students to not learn anything at all. Worse, would be for the student to believe he or she was not simply the root cause for the failure but the failure itself. I witnessed this happen once with a teacher I will call Ms. Meanypants.

School overcrowding is nothing new and art teachers are not always the first in line to be assigned a permanent room. Some art teachers are lucky and get a mobile unit. Other art teachers work miracles, going room to room teaching art on a cart. Still others find a way to share rooms during the main occupant's planning period. I experienced this situation early on in my career as I shared a science room.

The room I shared, though separated by a storage closet, was connected to another science room where Ms. Meanypants worked. Ms. Meanypants was strict, stern and never smiled. She liked things neat, orderly and quiet. I, on the other hand, was teaching art.

One afternoon, while I was talking to a team of students working on their noisy, collaborative group project, the storage closet door swung open. Ms. Meanypants bursts into the room and yelled, "Who is making that tapping sound!"

The class fell dead silent which was certainly a first for that group. Ms. Meanypants glared around the room. The kids were scared. I was scared.

Mike, one of the students I had just been speaking with, was the one to respond. Apparently, he had been bouncing on the floor, a piece of PVC piping his group was using for their project. I hadn't noticed at all. To me it was classic art room white noise but apparently it was very upsetting to Ms. Meanypants.

"My bad," he said, looked at the tubing. He then went on to explain how he was unconsciously taping the pipe and apologized again to Ms. Meanypants as the entire class listened in. This wasn't good enough for Ms. Meanypants. Instead of accepting Mike's apology, she lit into him. Still yelling, she explained how her class was trying to work. She added something about an inferno racket, having no respect and these kids today. Then, before anyone could say or do anything, she marched back into her room and slammed the door.

Mike felt terrible. You could tell by the look on his face. He had done everything right. He could have easily kept his mouth shut. Instead, he accepted responsibly for his actions. In front of the entire class, Mike announced that it was his fault, that he had been wrong and that he was sorry. He should have received an award of recognition for honesty and integrity. Instead, his reward was public humiliation and a tongue lashing.

Don't get me wrong. I'm not saying Ms. Meanypants didn't have a case. The conditions she deemed necessary for instructing her class were in direct opposition from mine. She had every right to come into the class, explain her situation and request us to pipe down (pun intended). Instead this became a failure in the true sense of the word. Not a failure of a project, or of the lesson, or of the student, but of an opportunity to demonstrate how to correctly handle a situation.

We won't succeed in every project we attempt no matter how prepared we think we are or how thorough our planning has been. There is nothing wrong with that. There is nothing wrong with failing. We need not only accept that as teachers, we need to explain that to our students. We need to allow them to make mistakes and to let them know that failing is perfectly all right. If you are like me, you'll go even one step further than letting your students know its ok to fail. You'll demonstrate it on fairly regular basis.

.....

Ian Sands

Book Two: The Story

Turning Teacher

Switching majors in college is not uncommon. Amateurs switch at least once. I, on the other hand was a professional. I switched majors from illustration to fine arts to toy design and finally landing back on illustration. Having switched so many times, I struggled my last year of college trying to pull together a portfolio. However, I ended up graduating with a decent set of illustration with a distinct style.

In the summer of 1989, with my illustration portfolio in tow, I hit the ground running. I made weekly trips into Manhattan to present my work at portfolio reviews. I sent hundreds of postcard to art directors. The results were always the same. Art directors liked my art but had no work for me right then. They would keep my postcard on file and let me know if anything came up. By the end of the summer I was discouraged, exhausted and worst of all, broke.

My friend Kevin offered me a solution. He worked for the Board Of Cooperative Services (BOCES). BOCES offered educational programs and services to school districts and was often in need of teacher assistants. Kevin suggested I take a job working as a teacher assistant while I pursued my illustration career. I could earn enough money to support myself and still have the afternoons free to drop off my portfolio. Kevin's plan seemed flawless. I applied, and was accepted for a position at an elementary class.

Do you remember your first day going to school as a child? There was that feeling of uncertainty, nervousness and dread. Being a grownup doesn't change that experience. I remember clearly stepping out of my car on my first day as a teacher assistant. Never being one to dress well, I wore a bad tie and a pair of uncomfortable shoes that matched the uncomfortableness I felt walking into that school. The kids all seemed like they knew what to do and where to go. All I could think was, "What am I doing here?"

The classroom set up wasn't anything different from how I remember my fourth grade classroom. There was a blackboard at the front of the class, there were little chairs and little desks for the little kids and there was a big chair and a big desk for me. I sat at my desk. I arranged the papers on my desk. I open the draw full of paperclips and staples. This wasn't so bad. Then the kids came in.

The kids were kids. They were funny looking. Their backpacks were too big. They smelled funny like all kids do. They sat at their desks like I sat at mine and we all waited for the teacher, Ms. Fraher, to tell us what to do.

Ms. Fraher was great. She was so organized and structured. She was really good at all those things I would have learned about in college if I hadn't dropped my Intro To Education class. But, since I had dropped that class, I had no idea how she knew what she was doing. So I asked her and she told me. It was then that I thought, writing a lesson plan might be sort of fun.

What was even more fun than planning lessons was being in school with the kids. This was in direct opposition to the drudgery of lugging my portfolio down to another art director so I could be rejected again. The more I was around the classroom, the less I wanted to commute to NYC. I remembered seeing a poster that was taped to the walls when I attended SVA. It read something like, "With your BFA and 15 credits in education you can become an art teacher." The idea grew like a seed that had been planted a few years before. I had my BFA. 15 credits couldn't be that hard to get. Again, my friend Kevin had a solution. Work towards getting your Masters at the College of New Rochelle.

Ian Sands

College Again?

The College of New Rochelle was certainly different than SVA. The graffiti scribbled city walls were replaced with bricks and ivory. The stacks of canvas and smells of oil paint and turpentine were replaced with the odor of stale library books.

I entered the dean's cramped office and sat in the small chair on the other side of her desk. Peering through her bifocals she asked, "Why do you want to become an educator."

Without hesitation, I blurted out the first thing that came to mind. "Cause, its fun!"

The dean burst out laughing. Then she collected her composure as she realized I was serious. In hindsight I'm sure she was looking for a more academic response. After all, most of the students attending her program already had an undergraduate understanding of education. I, on the other hand, had a pretty good idea of how to stretch a canvas and that was about it.

Despite my lack of education, I was accepted into the program and in 1990 I started my post baccalaureate studies in Art Education. Wow, was that ever boring! Whatever ill feelings I had for the Intro To Education class at SVA was nothing in comparision. This was ten times worse. We spent hours in the library reviewing microfiche of papers written by academics that lacked a certain anything. The papers were beyond dry and boring and what was worse, seemed to have no relevance to what I wanted to do which of course, was to teach.

Worse than the time spent in the library was the studio class. At least SVA had the good sense to take us to an elementary school were we could watch real children in action. New Rochelle provided no such opportunity. Instead, the instructor acted the part of an elementary teacher and we, the 21 year old students, played the role of the elementary kids.

"Today, we are going to draw different types of lines," the teacher instructed her class. We were each handed a pencil and a piece of paper divided into six boxes. "Draw a different type of line in each box."

In the first box I drew a telephone line. In the second box I drew a hungry lion. In the third box I drew an angry lion. When the instructor inspected my paper she was not pleased. I was a little indignatious. Wouldn't a kid who was frustrated by such a lame assignment act out in the same manor? I should have been award an A for the class. Instead I was reprimanded and told to draw the type of lines I was supposed to be drawing. I acquiesced and drew the most lack luster zig zag lines you ever saw.

I can't say I excelled at any part of my New Rochelle experience. I plodded through. It probably won't come as a surprise to learn I didn't finish the program. I stayed long enough to fulfill my teaching certificate requirements. 15 credits just like the poster stated. I didn't want to hang around any longer than I had to. I had a vision of being an art teacher. The idea of teaching as a means of making money until I could support myself selling my art was long gone. I wanted to be in a class room with real students working on real lessons, teaching art.

I Got The Job!

In 1990, New York was not hurting for art teachers. I
went on one interview where I was informed that 70 other
people had applied for the position. Meanwhile my older
brother had taken part in what was becoming the great
southern migration. He had moved to the suburbs of
Raleigh, NC. I was invited down to visit his new home
for Easter. North Carolina needed teachers. New York
did not. So, in June of 1990, with just enough money to
survive the summer, my wife to be and I moved to
Raleigh.

The plan was simple. Find a teaching job in the next three
months or return home with my tail between my legs. I
signed a short term lease for a one bedroom apartment.
Every Sunday, I would spread out the help wanted section
of the News and Observer across the carpet. For two
months I highlighted open positions and mailed resumes.
Half way through the third month I was offered an

interview for a middle school position in Sampson County.

Never being one to dress well, I went to Belk's and bought a new white shirt and pair of red suspenders. I drove an hour south till I reached the small central office building for Sampson County Schools in Clinton, NC. The interview went off without a hitch and I was offered the job. I later learned that I was hired because of the red suspenders. "When you showed up for an interview in Sampson County wearing those big red suspenders," Ms. Royal, principal of Roseboro-Salemburg Middle School told me. "I knew you were the right man for the job." I accepted the position.

The population of New York City in 1990 was close to nine million. The combined population of Roseboro and Salemburg, the two feeder towns for the middle school, was under 2,000. To say the least this was culture shock. As a native New Yorker, never having grown up in the south,there were some things I had never encountered.

On the good side there was barbecue, collard greens and fatback. On the bad side, sand spurs and fire ants. I had never seen a cotton field, smelled curing tobacco or lived in a county that was home to more pigs than people. I had also never coached football, never played football and rarely watched football on TV. This didn't stop my principal from assigning me the title of assistant football coach. After all, besides the head coach, I was the only other male teacher at the school.

Between all three grades, 6-8, I taught 400 kids a year. That number was equal to the amount of dollars in my budget. My principal was extremely supportive, often taking me on supply room raids. Still, things were tight. The lack of supplies forced me to be creative. I took amble advantage of any sort of technology I could get my hands on. The media center had video cameras so I established a weekly news program called Good Morning RSMS. Each week one of my classes had the responsibility of producing the show. We needed everything from reporters to camera operators to set designers and anchors. We would edit the tapes on Thursday and air it during homeroom every Friday morning.

Not everyone was so sure about what the boy from New York City was up to. After a lesson on sidewalk chalk, one teacher complained that I was teaching the students graffiti. The cafeteria staff wanted my head when a group of eighth graders created an installation called the Ten Commandments of the Lunch Room. They had designed ten tablet-shaped pieces of paper with sayings like, "Thou Show Not Complain About The Green Bologna". I apologized profusely and, to my student's dismay, uninstalled the installation.

Although I was having the time of my life, things weren't going as well back at home. Though I assimilated quickly into the southern way of life, my wife was growing more and more home sick every day. The birth of my first son and the thought of being away from family at such a time only heightened the desire. So after working in Sampson

County for four years we decided to pack it up and return home to New York. But you know what they say... You can never go home again.

Ian Sands

Learning The Web

It was my friend Kevin who once again set me on my future path. Back in New York there was a Technology Facilitator position opening in the department where he worked at BOCES. Basically, I would travel from school to school, inquire about the technology needs of the classroom and then return the following week to fulfill those requests. I applied, was accepted and in the summer of 1994 my family and I packed up our NC house and moved into a tiny apartment in Northern Westchester County.

To make good as a Technology Facilitator, I dove head first into the technology of the day. I purchased a top of the line Macintosh computer which, by today's standards would be the equivalent of a digital watch. The Internet was just taking root. Not many people were online yet and those who were connected through AOL using a dial up modem. Photoshop 2.0 was released and came on two floppy disks. This was a whole new world of art to me. It wasn't painting or drawing, but it was creating like it had never been done before.

One afternoon, my director came into the room and informed me that he wanted our department to have a webpage. Since I knew Photoshop, I should build it.

That weekend I found a magazine on the rack of a local Walmart titled Net Magazine. The feature article was about learning HTML. I purchased that magazine and spent the rest of the weekend learning to build webpages. Even back then, I knew this article would be life altering. I kept it as a memento and still have it today.

I didn't much enjoy being a Technology Facilitator but I very much enjoyed creating computer art and designing websites. I learned enough PhotoShop, HTML and a multimedia program called Macromedia Director to create an interactive portfolio. That fall, when BOCES needed a computer graphics instructor, I submitted my digital resume.

The Communications Academy was more or less a tech school for the arts. They offered Commercial Art and TV Production and were looking to expand the program with the addition of Computer Art and Web Design. The concept was exciting. Students enrolled in the Academy would be involved in all three subject areas. Many of the projects were designed to be collaborative between the three classes. For example, teams of students might be tasked with designing the packaging for a new brand of cereal in the Art class and then film a commercial in the TV Production class. The addition of a Computer Art class would open the doors for students to design those packages in Photoshop or create a webpage for their team's product. In theory everything was designed to be very collaborative, both at the student level and also the teacher level... or as we would say today, very PLC (Personal learning Community). Unfortunately, sometimes things that sound good in theory don't work out in reality.

The first issue was that no students were enrolled in my computer class. The premise was that I would periodically remove students from other classes so they could work in the lab. However, randomly pulling students, having no set schedule and loosely structured lesson plans, made it challenging for both myself and the other teachers. It was an awkward situation that became stressful at times. Though I was there to collaborate, many of the plans had already been developed. Instead of being part of the plan, my role was seen more as an add-on and not always a welcomed one.

Perhaps most ironic was my inability to communicate with my fellow teachers at the Communications Academy. I can recall several failed attempts where what I was trying to convey either came out wrong or was misinterpreted. Sometime both occurred simultaneously. Whether it was the situation or my inability to express myself, it was becoming clear that I was not the right fit for this team.

During this time, two things were taking shape. First, like nearly half of all teachers that leave the profession in the first five years, I was burning out. Instead of using my time to plan lessons and create new projects, I was honing my web designing skills. On the weekends, I would stay up half the night banging out lines of code. I started to question why, if coding was what I did in my spare time, I couldn't find a job doing it for a living.

Second, my wife and I were quickly coming to the realization that you can never go home again. The promise of being closer to family was only a pipe dream. The long winters and higher taxes reminded us of why we left NY in the first place. We had done it before, we could certainly do it again. This time however, it would be different. Instead of returning to the country life of Sampson County, we would relocate to the City of Raleigh. Instead of a low paying teaching position, I would find a high wage career as a web designer.

Ian Sands

The Boss

If you've ever watched the movie Office Space than you will understand what my life was like for the next five years. The movie is a comedy about a group of IT workers that deal with the ridiculousness of working for a tech company called Initech. The main charter, Peter Gibbons, has pointless paper work to track and meaningless tasks to perform. Worse than that, Peter is constantly harassed by his five bosses. Though the movie is a satire, from my experience, it is based on facts. Though Initech is an imaginary company, to me it was all too real. Even though one of Peter's bosses, Bill Lumbergh, is a fictional character, I have a good feeling I know who he is modeled after.

My sister in law once told me, you will have good managers and you will have bad managers. What I came to understand is that there are two types of bosses in the world. This applied to mangers and principals and probably teachers too. The first type of boss views the employee as the expert. They hired their employees to perform jobs that they themselves cannot do. They value their employees and realize that a rising tide lifts all boats.

My project manager at Nortel, where I worked as a web designer, was this type of boss. He realized that if I went from being a web designer to being a project manger then he would go from being a project manager to being a manager. These are the types of bosses you want to work with.

The second type of boss views his employees as work horses. This type of boss is really only interested in himself and his self promotion. The only thing that matter is that you do what you are told. After all, this person is the boss.

After leaving Nortel, I took a position as a graphical user interface designer for a company similar to Initech. To protect the innocent and as a tribute to Office Space I'll refer to the company as Outitech.

My boss at Outitech viewed his employees as workhorses. I can only assume he saw me as a wild stallion in need of discipline. He would surely break the spirit of this noble beast and bring him inline. Unfortunately for this boss, I was what horse people might call unbreakable.

Before I tell you about my encounters with this boss, I need to explain a little bit about what was going on inside my head prior to the events. In my heart I knew I missed teaching. I would watch PBS on Friday nights. They ran a program where students from local schools would discuss classes and outstanding projects they were working on. I would watch this show and ask myself, why am I not doing this? At night, I started searching job listings for teaching positions. I got all my paper work together, just in case.

Meanwhile at work, my boss's favorite pastime was finding ways to breath down my neck. I remember one day I was sick as a dog but since I had some graphics to make, I decide to go to work in spite of my illness. The longer I stayed, the worse I felt but I still managed to created all the graphics needed for the day.

At five o'clock I walked out the back door and headed to my car. Halfway between the door and my car I heard a voice ask, "Where are you going?"

I turned around and saw it was my boss.

"I'm going home," I replied. "I'm sick."

"Well," said my boss. "You're suppose to work till 5:30." Then he paused. I stood in the parking lot with a fever that had set in, waiting for his response. Finally he added, "Well, I guess if you're sick, you can go."

I went home and updated my resume.

The final straw came several months later. I had changed roles from Graphic Designer to Product Trainer. My boss wanted me to go to Chicago to teach a new guy the system. I knew I could train this guy in a day. I also knew, since I was playing on a hockey league, that I had a hockey game on Wednesday night. I concluded that I should go to Chicago for two days and be home by Wednesday for the game. My boss had other plans. He called me into his office and said, "I see you have only scheduled a two day trip to Chicago. I need you to go for the entire week."

I had two problems with this. First, I knew it wouldn't take a week to train the new guy. Second, I had a hockey game on Wednesday night.

If I had truly needed to go to Chicago for a week, I would have. But that length of time was unnecessary. Furthermore, my boss knew it was unnecessary. This wasn't about the time it would take for the training. This was a showdown. My boss was giving me an order and I had better follow it. Not because it was right or reasonable or cost effective for the company, but for his own egotistical reasons.

We went back and forth. I tried to explain why such a long trip was unnecessary, he held firm to unreason. Finally I was threatened, "You can either go to Chicago for a week or you can turn in your resignation."

I went directly to HR. Apparently, after all the work I had successfully complete for Outitech, HR didn't think this situation was grounds to fire me. HR helped mediated a compromise. I would go to Chicago for three day. This was fine by me. I would train the new guy and still be home by Wednesday night in time to play my hockey game. It's about priorities, right?

Then a funny thing happened. I received a call from Apex high School. They wanted me to come in for an interview. I explained that I was going to Chicago but would be back Thursday. We scheduled the interview.

So that Monday I boarded a plane for Chicago. I trained the new guy and in two days he had it down pat. I flew home Wednesday afternoon and went directly from the airport to the ice rink. I don't remember if my team won of lost that night but I'm going to say we won. Thursday, I met with the principal of Apex High School. The interview went swimmingly. On Friday morning, I received a job offer. Friday afternoon I told my boss he could kiss my... I mean, I thanked him for the opportunity to have worked at Outitech but I had accepted the position as Art Teacher for Apex High School.

Ian Sands

ABOUT THE AUTHOR

I wasn't sure what to write about myself so I ask my students at Apex High what should go here. Here is what they said...

Ian Sands loves the Jersey Shore, even though he's never actually watched it. He likes squirting students with his water gun even when they aren't talking. He likes blowing bubbles out of his Jeep while driving. He has a healthy obsession with tin foil, and doesn't own a single pair of paint-less pants. He loves the Venus of Willendorf and zonkeys. He makes such great lunches and really appreciates a good scone.

Made in the USA
Middletown, DE
17 January 2021